Drug Abuse and Society™

ROHYPNOL
Roofies—"The Date Rape Drug"

The Rosen Publishing Group, Inc., New York

Colleen Adams

Published in 2007 by The Rosen Publishing Group, Inc.
29 East 21st Street, New York, NY 10010

Library of Congress Cataloging-in-Publication Data

Adams, Colleen.
Rohypnol: roofies—"the date rape drug" / Colleen Adams.—1st ed.
   p. cm.—(Drug abuse and society)
Includes bibliographical references and index.
ISBN-13: 978-1-4042-0914-5 (library binding)
ISBN-10: 1-4042-0914-X (library binding)
1. Flunitrazepam—Social aspects. 2. Date rape drugs—Social aspects.
I. Title. II. Series.
RM666.F52A33 2007
362.883—dc22

                                2006008490

Manufactured in the United States of America

Contents

INTRODUCTION

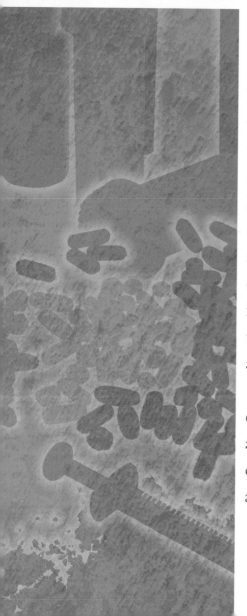

Drug abuse is a major threat to our communities today. For teens, peer pressure and the many other challenges of growing up may influence them to experiment with drugs. They may think that they won't become addicted, or that long-term drug use will not be harmful. However, substance abuse can cause life-threatening health problems, as well as physical and psychological dependence. Other negative consequences include failing grades, loss of income, and unstable relationships with family members and friends.

Besides the risk of death from overdose, drug abuse exposes the user to being arrested or becoming a victim of a violent crime. In addition, studies show that teens are more likely to have unprotected sex while under the influence of drugs. This unsafe behavior could result in a sexually transmitted disease or in an unwanted pregnancy. Monitoring the Future is an annual survey conducted by the National Institute on Drug Abuse. It gathers information about drug, alcohol, and cigarette use among adolescents across the nation. In 2005, more than 49,300 students in the eighth, tenth, and twelfth grades participated in the survey. Results showed that half of these students had used at least one illegal drug before graduating from high school. The survey also showed that teenagers' use of prescription drugs was increasing. One drug included in the survey was Rohypnol, a strong sedative, or calming drug, that has not been approved for medical use or sale in the United States. Although only a small percentage of teens reported using Rohypnol, the drug still presents serious dangers. This book describes those dangers and explains how to avoid them.

Rohypnol is the brand name for flunitrazepam, a man-made drug belonging to a class of drugs called benzodiazepines. Benzodiazepine drugs are depressants—drugs that act on the central nervous system, slowing the user's heart rate, breathing, and thought processes. Rohypnol is similar in chemical content to Valium, a commonly prescribed benzodiazepine sedative; however, Rohypnol is ten times stronger than Valium. First manufactured by the Swiss pharmaceutical company Hoffman-LaRoche, Rohypnol is widely available by prescription in Europe and Latin America. It is used to treat people who have severe difficulty falling asleep, and it is sometimes given to sedate patients before surgery. Even when used according to directions, Rohypnol can decrease blood pressure and cause dizziness, disorientation, slurred speech, loss of motor coordination, impaired judgment, stomach problems, sleepiness, blackouts, and memory loss. The drug acts quickly, within thirty minutes after it is taken, and its effects may last for eight to twelve hours or longer.

The relatively low cost of Rohypnol—less than $5 a pill—and its wide availability made it a popular street drug in the United States in the early 1990s. Most users at that time took Rohypnol to enhance the effects of marijuana or heroin. Some took it to ease the depression of "coming down" from a cocaine high. More recently, Rohypnol has become a popular drug among young people attending dance parties and clubs. Users typically combine Rohypnol with other drugs, including ecstasy (MDMA), GHB, and ketamine. These drugs, known as "club drugs," are attractive to some teens because they are cheap and their effects are intense. Combining these drugs, however, may cause hallucinations, paranoia, amnesia, and, in some cases, death.

Rohypnol is tasteless and odorless, and it can be dissolved easily in a drink. Even a small dose of one milligram can affect a person for eight hours or longer. By the mid-1990s, these qualities made Rohypnol a popular drug used by men to sedate unsuspecting victims in sexual assaults. The drug acts quickly and causes victims to feel highly intoxicated and extremely confused. As Rohypnol also causes blackouts and memory loss, especially if combined with alcohol, victims are often unable to remember clear and accurate details of an assault. This makes it difficult for victims to give credible information that may be used to prosecute the person guilty of the assault. Today, Rohypnol's dangers are rather well known among young people. Nevertheless, the drug remains popular in some circles, especially in the American Southwest, near the U.S.-Mexico border.

CHAPTER 1
Rohypnol in America and the Rise of Club Drugs

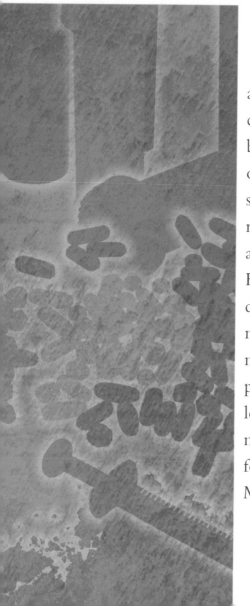

Rohypnol has been on the market for more than thirty years. It is prescribed legally in Europe, Mexico, and Central and South America. However, due to its potential for abuse, it has never been approved for use in the United States or Canada. Rohypnol is the third most prescribed sleeping medication in the world, related to such widely prescribed benzodiazepine drugs as Valium, Librium, and Xanax. For many years, doctors have used these drugs effectively in the treatment of insomnia, seizures, and anxiety disorders. These medications have calming effects when used properly on a short-term basis. The problem with benzodiazepine drugs is that users may develop an addiction if they take them for a long time or in the wrong dosage. Many who take Rohypnol think it is safe

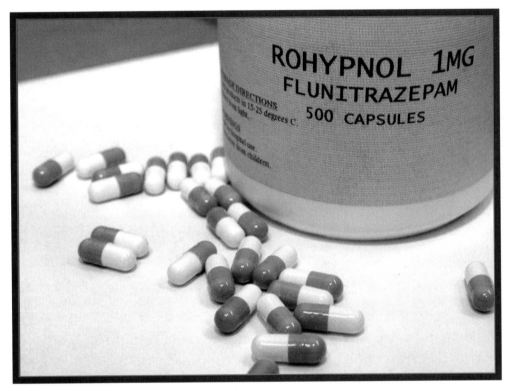

This bottle of Rohypnol pills was confiscated in Finland in 2003. In the drug bust, authorities seized more than 400,000 Rohypnol pills, as well as materials for making an additional 1 million pills. The trafficking of Rohypnol, both legal and illegal, is a global issue.

to use because of its similarity to the other legal, widely used drugs. However, Rohypnol has a much higher potency than the other benzodiazepine drugs and may have dangerous side effects.

MISLEADING DRUG ADVERTISING

Until the 1990s, drug companies tended to focus on only the positive aspects of benzodiazepine drugs and their ability to give patients relief from tension and stress. As a result, doctors around the world often overprescribed these medications. Some users became so dependent on benzodiazepine drugs that they felt unable to cope with normal, everyday stress without them. In light of this, health and consumer organizations criticized pharmaceutical (drug) companies, claiming that their advertising was misleading. These advocacy groups stated that drug companies did not provide enough information about the negative effects of their benzodiazepine drugs, which can be highly addictive and may cause severe depression if taken with alcohol. Responding to the criticism, in the mid-1990s, some drug companies advertised their products more responsibly. Consumers were better informed, but the demand for benzodiazepine drugs remained high.

ILLEGAL DISTRIBUTION OF ROHYPNOL

By the late 1980s, there were reports of Rohypnol distribution and abuse in the states of Florida, Arizona, California, and Texas. By 1995, the U.S. Drug Enforcement Administration (DEA) had documented more than 1,000 cases of Rohypnol possession in thirteen states. The two largest seizures of Rohypnol took place in 1995, when shipments of more than 50,000 tablets were confiscated in Louisiana and Texas.

In the early 1990s, it was not difficult to bring drugs such as Rohypnol into the United States. As Rohypnol was legal in Mexico, people simply crossed the U.S.–Mexico border, legally

Illegal drug trafficking is a problem at the U.S.-Mexico border. It is impossible to inspect all of the thousands of vehicles that enter the United States every day at the border crossing at Tijuana, Mexico *(above)*. International mail services are also used to smuggle Rohypnol into the United States.

purchased the drugs in Mexico, and came back. Customs officials allowed U.S. citizens to bring the drugs into the United States as long as they had a Mexican prescription for them. The problem was that illegal drug traffickers, too, were buying Rohypnol and other drugs in Mexico and bringing them into the United States.

ROHYPNOL'S REPUTATION TAKES A TURN

On the street, Rohypnol pills became known as "rophies," "roach" (or "Roche"), and "roofies." Before long, the drug also began receiving attention for reasons other than its risk of addiction. Reports from around the country said that men were using it to render women unconscious in order to assault them sexually. Rohypnol's use for this purpose—as a "date rape drug"—forced authorities to take a tougher stance on controlling its availability and distribution.

In 1996, the U.S. government changed some of its customs laws. It officially prohibited the importation of Rohypnol, whether a person had a prescription or not. However, the drug continued to be brought in from countries where it was legal. By August 1997, Rohypnol use had been reported in thirty-eight states.

Nationally, the use of Rohypnol seemed to be spreading. But the government reported that it was succeeding in its efforts to limit the drug's availability. For example, DEA records showed that the agency seized more than 160,000 illegal Rohypnol doses in 1995. By 2000, however, the DEA reported that traffic of Rohypnol across the U.S.-Mexico border was slowing to a trickle; that year, the agency seized a mere 4,967 doses.

DANGEROUS CLUB DRUGS

Although DEA reports indicated a decrease in Rohypnol trafficking between 1995 and 2000, the drug was becoming quite popular as a "club drug" or "fun drug." Club drugs are used to enhance the atmosphere at raves (all-night dance parties), bars, and clubs. Raves are usually held in secret places such as old warehouses. They feature DJs playing loud, pulsating music; partiers often wear outlandish and sexy costumes. Some who attend raves say that club drugs give them the stamina to party all night, and also make social interaction easier.

The most popular club drugs include ecstasy, GHB, Rohypnol, and ketamine. Club drugs are easy for teens to use because they are relatively inexpensive and usually come in the form of pills, liquids, or powders.

Ecstasy (MDMA)

Also known as "X," "E," and "roll," ecstasy (MDMA) is a chemical substance usually taken in pill form. It is a stimulant and a

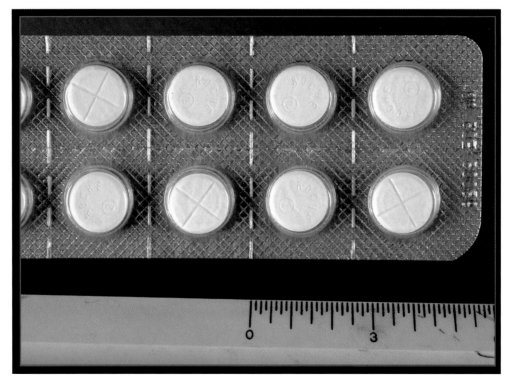

Ecstasy is usually purchased in individual, unwrapped doses. Rohypnol, on the other hand, can be bought off the street in blister packs like those shown here. Users may be fooled into thinking that Rohypnol isn't dangerous because it is packaged like other prescription drugs.

hallucinogen. Club drug users say they take ecstasy because it makes them happy and gives them energy to dance.

Ecstasy affects the brain's chemistry. It increases the levels of serotonin, a chemical messenger, giving the user a joyful, carefree feeling that lasts four to six hours. The side effects are rapid heart rate, loss of appetite, jaw tension, teeth grinding, and sweating. Ecstasy users risk dehydration, a condition that occurs when the body loses a lot of water—through sweating, for instance—that is not replaced. More serious side effects include hyperthermia (dangerously high body temperature) and heart or kidney failure. Ecstasy may cause dangerous psychological effects for weeks after taking it. These effects include depression, sleep problems, severe anxiety and paranoia, hallucinations, and violent and irrational behavior. Taking ecstasy over a long period may cause permanent damage to parts of the brain that are critical for memory.

GHB (Gamma Hydroxybutyrate)

GHB is an anabolic steroid, a type of muscle-building chemical. It is also a powerful central nervous system depressant. Also, known as "G," "Gina," and "Georgia Home Boy," it comes as a pure liquid or in powder form that is easily dissolved in liquid. During the 1980s, bodybuilders could buy GHB over the counter to help them lose weight and build muscle. In 1990, however, the U.S. Food and Drug Administration (FDA) banned using this drug without a doctor's supervision. Today, it is made illegally in secret labs and sold as a club drug known for its sedative effect.

GHB is made from chemicals that are also ingredients used to make paint stripper, plastics, and adhesives. The drug takes effect within thirty minutes after ingestion and lasts for three to five hours. At doses of up to two grams, GHB can cause drowsiness, decreased heart and breathing rates, and impaired motor control.

A club drug user is shown playing with glow sticks at an all-night rave. Club drugs enhance the effects of sights and sounds for the user. They may also give the user a feeling of high energy and alertness. But the combination of stimulation and physical exertion puts dangerous amounts of stress on the user's body and mind.

GHB is dangerous because users may not be aware of the harmful chemicals that have been combined to make it. Alcohol enhances the depressant effects of this drug. Overdosing on GHB can severely decrease your breathing rate, and can lead to unconsciousness, coma, and even death.

Ketamine (Ketamine Hydrochloride)

Ketamine, another popular club drug, is a central nervous system depressant that reduces pain perception and causes sedation. It is also known as "K," "Special K," "Vitamin K," and "Kit Kat." Ketamine was developed in the 1970s as an anesthetic mainly used by veterinarians. In its powder form, it can be snorted or sprinkled in tobacco or marijuana cigarettes. It is sometimes injected directly into muscles. The effects of ketamine may include slurred speech, increased or otherwise abnormal heart rate, increased blood pressure, lack of coordination, paralysis, and respiratory problems. A person under the influence of ketamine may appear to be in a dreamlike state. A user may have some or all of the following reactions: hallucinations, paranoia, aggressive behavior, and impaired memory. The effects of a typical dose (about 40 mg) of ketamine may last from one to six hours.

CHAPTER 2
The Dangers of Club Drugs

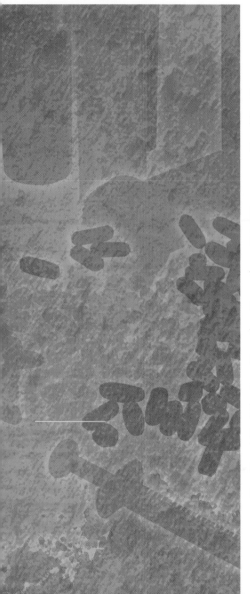

Drugs like ecstasy, Rohypnol, GHB, and ketamine stimulate and depress the central nervous system. In combination, they can cause extreme physical and psychological reactions that may result in long-term damage to the body.

REASONS FOR USING DRUGS

When users take club drugs, they do not always know how and where the drugs were manufactured. Dealers often substitute another drug without the user's knowledge, so users are unaware of the exact kind and amount of chemicals they are ingesting. Users who combine club drugs are putting themselves at high risk for permanent brain damage, overdose, and death.

Why do teens still take club drugs when there are so many associated health and safety risks? There are many factors involved in triggering drug use. Some teens may take drugs simply because it makes them feel good. Others may think that drugs help them deal with the stress of keeping up with demands at home, school, and their jobs. Some may be curious about how the drugs will make them feel. Others may use drugs as a way to fit in with a certain peer group. Still others may take

Teen Drug Use: The Numbers

Among students who took part in the 2005 Monitoring the Future (MTF) study conducted by the National Institute on Drug Abuse, 2.8 percent of eighth graders, 4 percent of tenth graders, and 5.4 percent of twelfth graders reported using ecstasy at least once in their lifetime. Comparison between 2004 and 2005 statistics showed that ecstasy use stayed the same for eighth graders, but went down for tenth and twelfth graders. Rohypnol use by eighth graders increased. Fortunately, its use was down among tenth and twelfth graders.

Rohypnol use is not as widespread as marijuana and cocaine use. According to the results of the 2005 MTF survey, 16.5 percent of eighth graders and 34.1 percent of tenth graders reported using marijuana at least once in their lifetime. Nearly 45 percent of twelfth graders who took part in the survey reported having used marijuana. In addition, the survey showed that 3.7 percent of eighth graders and 5.2 percent of tenth graders reported using cocaine sometime during their lifetime. About 8 percent of twelfth graders reported having used cocaine.

drugs to hide their fears or insecurities. Habitual users may think that they have to take drugs to have a good time. Most teens know the drugs they try can be harmful and addictive. But the more they use the drugs, the harder it is to stop.

KAREN'S STORY

Karen was a typical teen, but she always felt like she didn't fit in. She lived like typical teens do, in a nice home with her family, but like some of her friends, she found herself bored with her surroundings and day-to-day routine. She was unexcited by meeting her girlfriends on the weekends and going for a bite to eat and a movie. Soon, Karen began noticing some of the kids who were hanging out between classes at school. She would normally avoid these students because her friends had dubbed them the "stoner" crowd, but Karen was curious about their clique. She liked the way the girls dressed, and she noticed that there were always guys around them, too. These girls seemed to be getting more attention from the guys than she and her friends ever did. Karen began hanging around between classes, too. She was more straightlaced than this crowd, so she felt pressured to let her hair down a little to blend in.

An Invitation to Join

One morning, one of the "stoner" girls, Jeanie, asked Karen for a pen and they started talking. Karen was surprised when she found they had a lot in common. Jeanie suggested that she hang out with their group that afternoon down by the outdoor bleachers. Karen was excited. She knew that this invitation meant she was being accepted. There was only one problem: she also knew that being fully accepted meant that she would have to try whatever drugs were being used.

After the group had assembled, one of the boys lit a marijuana joint and started passing it around. Karen smiled and took a hit when it was her turn. She felt strangely at ease with the group and was thrilled to feel so welcomed. One of the guys, Tim, asked her if she'd like to go to a cool "secret" party, an all-night rave, on Saturday. Karen was so happy to be asked out—especially by Tim, who was considered one of the cutest guys in school.

At the rave, Tim suggested that he and Karen split a "roofie" (Rohypnol). When the drug took effect, Karen described her experience as "incredible. I felt so peaceful, and the music sounded great. I felt so relaxed with my new friends, like I had never felt before." Tim and Karen started dating and regularly attending raves. Before long, she was using an assortment of club drugs, including ecstasy.

Life Takes a Turn

Karen's first experiences using drugs left her feeling good. Naturally, she wanted to repeat that feeling over and over again. However, as she continued to take the same drugs for a few

The effects of club drugs can easily cause a user to pass out or "crash" for a long time. Often, users wake up unaware of where they are or how they got there. Although this young drug user looks peaceful now, he probably won't be feeling very well when he wakes up.

months, the good feeling she associated with them faded. She was building up a tolerance to the drugs. In order to get the same good feeling again, she had to increase the amount of the drug or take stronger drugs.

Karen noticed that the drugs began to affect the way she felt when she wasn't high. She often had headaches, which she never had before. During the day, she felt nauseated and depressed. Instead of feeling optimistic about her life, Karen started hating everything—school, her family, even her new friends. Her parents were always angry with her, and they wouldn't stop asking her what was wrong. She thought they had a problem with her being independent. This only made Karen more depressed. It seemed as if the only time she felt good was when she was taking drugs at parties.

A Birthday Nightmare

Everything changed on Karen's seventeenth birthday. Thinking that her special day would be a good time to try something new, Karen decided to combine three drugs she had previously taken individually—Rohypnol, ecstasy, and ketamine. She expected to have a great night, but she didn't know that the combination of drugs was too strong for her nervous system. Soon after taking them, she felt very cold, and her chest hurt. She tried to get up and dance it off, but as soon as she stood up, she lost her balance and fell to the floor. Karen's friends tried to help her stand, but she had lost consciousness. When she didn't wake up after a few minutes, her friends got scared and rushed her to the hospital.

The doctors at the hospital told Karen later that she had stopped breathing several times and had even slipped into a coma. Karen was fortunate to survive her terrible experience without any serious injuries. But she could no longer lie to herself and deny that she had a drug problem. Her parents helped her get into a drug-abuse recovery program, which helped her change her lifestyle.

It is important for a teen who has a drug problem to maintain—or re-establish—a relationship with parents and other loved ones. Talking about a drug problem with a parent or counselor can be the first step toward overcoming addiction.

Recovery, however, took a long time. Even with the help of counselors and the loving support of her parents, Karen constantly felt the temptation to return to using drugs.

Like Karen, many teens have had experiences in which using club drugs brought negative, dangerous, and life-threatening consequences. Even so, quitting is not easy. Overcoming a drug addiction brings its own share of physical and emotional pain. Drug-abusing teens often break off the normal, established relationships they share with parents and other family members. A drug abuser's preferred substance may become more important than anything or anyone else. When this happens, parents may feel as if they don't know who their child is or how to cope with the realities of the addiction.

CHAPTER 3

The Use of Rohypnol to Facilitate Sexual Assault

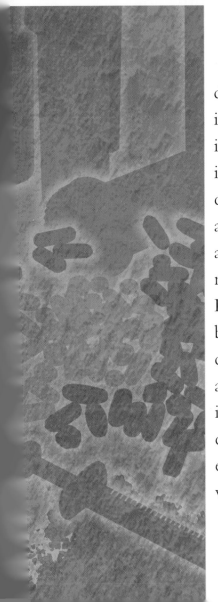

Rohypnol is recognized as a highly addictive drug. Since it is a fast-acting sedative, it is also extremely dangerous in the hands of people with bad intentions. The drug has been used in physical assaults, robberies, and sexual assaults to incapacitate victims so that a crime can be committed against them. Its use in sexual assaults earned Rohypnol a reputation as a "date rape drug," although that name is not entirely accurate. (See next page.) Rohypnol can be a criminal's best friend because it affects the memory, making it difficult for a victim to recall the details of a crime. Without accurate recollections, it is hard to prove what happened during a crime. Consequently, there is often not enough evidence to prosecute someone who is accused of such an assault.

HOW IS DATE RAPE DIFFERENT FROM DRUG-FACILITATED SEXUAL ASSAULT?

Sexual assault is an attack such as rape or attempted rape, as well as any unwanted sexual contact or threats. Rohypnol is commonly called a date rape drug. However, the type of sexual assault usually done with the aid of Rohypnol is technically not the same as date rape. In a date rape, the victim knows her attacker, and the assault usually occurs on a date. The victim is not drugged but is forced to have sex. In a drug-facilitated sexual assault, the victim may or may not know the person who assaults her. She is secretly given a drug that will prevent her from resisting a sexual assault. By law, both of these situations are sexual assaults because the victim does not give her consent to have sex.

Both females and males can be rendered helpless by Rohypnol. However, the great majority of victims of sexual assaults facilitated by Rohypnol are females of high school or college age.

CATHERINE'S STORY

Catherine's experience as a victim of a drug-facilitated sexual assault is very similar to those reported by many other young women who have called rape crisis centers for help.

Catherine went out with her friends to a college party. She had a couple drinks and met a few new people. When a new

26

A young woman alone in a club or at a bar may be a target for a sexual predator. Even if you go out with friends, you should never leave your drink unattended. It only takes a few seconds for someone to spike your drink with a drug.

acquaintance offered her a drink, she accepted it, thinking it was safe because she was among friends. This person, who Catherine knew only casually, spiked her drink with Rohypnol in order to sexually assault her. She could not see or taste anything unusual in her drink, and she did not know she had been drugged. The last thing she remembered about that night was taking a sip of her drink. The next morning, Catherine woke up in a house where some of the guys from the party lived. Her body was sore, and she knew that she had been sexually assaulted. The Rohypnol caused her to have amnesia, so she couldn't remember what happened to her.

HOW TO TELL IF A VICTIM HAS BEEN DRUGGED

The effects of Rohypnol may be different for each person. How much of the drug was taken and whether it was mixed with alcohol or other drugs are big factors. Catherine said that the last thing she remembered was taking sips of her drink. This is definitely a clue that Rohypnol or a similar drug was used; she was sedated quickly and blacked out. The next day, Catherine woke up in a strange place with a headache. She felt confused and could not remember how she got there or what happened. This experience is similar to those described by other Rohypnol victims. The drug causes them to forget events that happened while they were under its influence. Catherine knew that someone had sex with her without her consent, but she could not prove who it was. The confusion, loss of memory, and waking up in an unfamiliar place are all signs that Catherine had been drugged. She felt embarrassed and shocked that this had happened to her. While these are normal reactions to a traumatic event, it is important for victims to know that the assault was not their fault.

HOW TO HELP SOMEONE WHO MAY HAVE BEEN DRUGGED

If one of Catherine's friends had been looking out for her, she may have been able to get away before the sexual assault took place. It is very important to take care of yourself and watch out for your friends when going to parties and clubs. What should you do if you are at a party and you think a friend may have been drugged? First, your friend may be embarrassed, confused, or scared, so try to be calm and comforting. Then, take these steps to keep your friend safe:

- Stay with your friend and make sure she is in a safe place.
- Do not allow her to "sleep it off" or stay somewhere alone.
- Call 911 or take your friend to a hospital immediately for help.

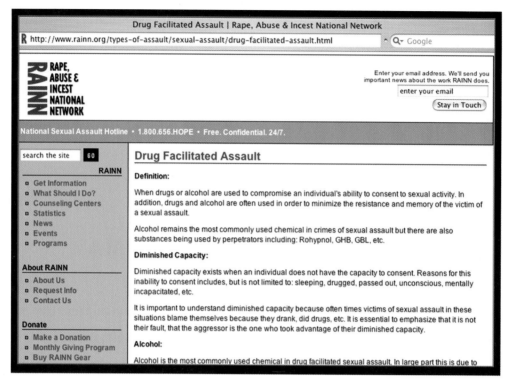

The Rape, Abuse and Incest National Network (RAINN) maintains the National Sexual Assault Hotline: 1-800-656-HOPE (1-800-656-4673). Victims of sexual assault can call the number round the clock to receive free advice. The hotline has served more than 900,000 sexual assault victims since it was created in 1994.

WHAT HAPPENS AFTER A SEXUAL ASSAULT?

Unfortunately, it is difficult for the victim to prove that a sexual assault occurred when the effects of the drug interfere with her ability to remember the details. In many cases, a victim will not report a drug-facilitated assault because of shock, embarrassment, or confusion. One of the few ways to prove that a drug was used in a sexual assault is through a urine test. Rohypnol stays in a person's body up to seventy-two hours. If it is detected in a urine test, it may be used as evidence against the person accused of a crime.

A drug-facilitated sexual assault puts the victim at risk of getting pregnant. It also puts her at risk of contracting AIDS (acquired immunodeficiency syndrome) or other sexually transmitted diseases. For these reasons, it is important for a victim to call a local rape crisis center or the police as soon as possible after an assault to get medical and legal assistance.

Health care professionals and law enforcement agencies are trained to take date rape reports seriously and to help the victim gather evidence. The reaction to the trauma of a sexual assault varies from woman to woman. Talking to a professional counselor can help the victim express and deal with her emotions, which may include feeling out of control, angry, depressed, or withdrawn. Offering support and understanding to a victim will help in her recovery process.

PREVENTION: HOW TO KEEP FROM BECOMING A VICTIM

There are many ways you can protect yourself and your friends when going to a club or party to make sure that everyone stays safe.

How to Get Help If You Are the Victim of a Drug-Facilitated Assault

- Call a friend or family member to come and be with you.
- Call 911 to report the assault to the police immediately. There is limited time to test for the presence of Rohypnol or other date rape drugs.
- Go to a hospital or rape crisis center right away. Do not bathe or change clothes before going to a hospital or clinic.
- Give a urine sample as soon as possible to have it tested for Rohypnol or other date rape drugs.
- Consider filing charges against the person you suspect gave you the drug and assaulted you. Write down anything you remember about the person you think was responsible for the assault, like hair color, height, weight, clothing, skin color, etc.
- Get help and support such as counseling. Call a crisis hot-line and seek crisis-intervention counseling or therapy.
- To find the rape crisis center closest to you, call the twenty-four-hour National Sexual Assault Hotline operated through the Rape, Abuse and Incest National Network (RAINN) at 1-800-656-HOPE.

- Never leave your drink unattended.
- Be aware of your surroundings and be able to identify the effects of date rape drugs.
- Do not accept drinks, including soda or water, from someone you don't know well and trust.
- Do not share or exchange drinks with anyone.

- Do not take a drink from a punch bowl or any open containers.
- Always go to a party with friends. Check on them often.
- Do not drink anything that has a funny smell, color, or taste. GHB may taste salty. New Rohypnol pills turn liquids a cloudy blue. However, the old white tablets are still available.
- Be aware that date rape drugs are most often disguised in alcoholic drinks, even though they can also be put in non-alcoholic drinks.

CHAPTER 4

Rohypnol, Club Drugs, and the Legal System

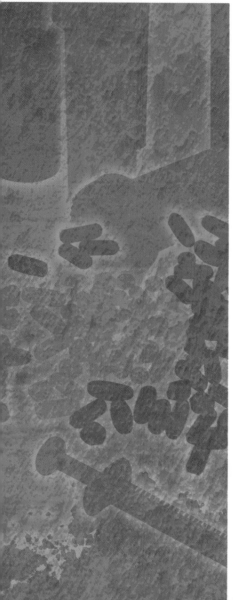

Chapters 1 and 2 discussed how club drugs like Rohypnol can be harmful to one's health and are highly addictive. These issues of health and addiction are very private, personal problems. However, the consequences of drug use are not limited to personal dangers. Using Rohypnol or other drugs may also bring with it serious legal consequences, which are played out in public.

U.S. LAWMAKERS RESPOND TO THE DANGERS OF ROHYPNOL

To address the growing problem of drug-facilitated sexual assault, the U.S. Congress passed the Drug-Induced Rape Prevention and Punishment Act in 1996. This legislation increased federal criminal penalties for the use of any controlled substance, including Rohypnol, to aid in a violent crime.

According to this law, simply possessing Rohypnol can result in up to three years in prison and a fine. Giving Rohypnol to another person without his or her knowledge is a serious offense. If it is done with the intent to commit a crime of violence, a person can be sentenced for up to twenty years and be fined. The new law also imposes a penalty of up to twenty years for the distribution and importation of one gram or more of Rohypnol.

Rohypnol and the Drug-Induced Rape Prevention and Punishment Act of 1996

Crime	Imprisonment
• Possession of Rohypnol	Three years maximum
• Giving someone Rohypnol with the intention of committing a crime	Twenty years maximum
• Importing or exporting Rohypnol	Twenty years maximum
• Causing injury or death to someone by giving them Rohypnol	Twenty years minimum/life

MYTHS AND FACTS ABOUT ROHYPNOL

Myth: Rohypnol pills are packaged as prescription drugs, so they must be safe and legal.

Fact: Rohypnol is an illegal drug in the United States and is commonly used to facilitate a sexual assault, making it extremely dangerous in the wrong hands.

Myth: You will know if someone puts Rohypnol in your drink.

Fact: Original-formula Rohypnol is tasteless and odorless, making it almost impossible to detect in a drink.

Myth: Rohypnol and Valium are essentially the same drug.

Fact: Although both Rohypnol and Valium are benzodiazepine drugs, there are significant differences. Rohypnol's effects and potency are ten times stronger than Valium. Rohypnol is not legal in the United States. Valium is a legal prescription drug.

Myth: You can control what happens to you while under the influence of Rohypnol.

Fact: Rohypnol depresses or slows down your central nervous system. It can cause confusion, loss of coordination and reasoning abilities, blackouts, and loss of memory of events that happened while under the influence.

ROHYPNOL AND DRUG CLASSIFICATION

It is the federal government's responsibility to protect the health and general welfare of American citizens. To this end, the U.S. Congress passed the Controlled Substances Act in 1970. This legislation requires the government to closely monitor the use of both legal and illegal drugs. The two government bodies involved in these efforts are the Drug Enforcement Administration (DEA), which is within the Department of Justice, and the Food and Drug Administration (FDA), which is within the Department of Health and Human Services. Together, these agencies classify and control pharmaceuticals and other drugs. The different classifications, called schedules, determine the legality of a substance and describe how it must be used and monitored.

There are five schedules of drug classifications. Schedule I is the most restrictive, and Schedule V is the least restrictive. In 1984, Rohypnol was added to Schedule IV. Drugs under this schedule are thought to have a low potential for abuse. They also have an accepted medical use for treatment in the United States. Although the FDA never approved it for the U.S. market, Rohypnol has remained a Schedule IV drug. In 1997, however, the U.S. Sentencing Commission further increased the penalties associated with Rohypnol possession and distribution. So, although the drug is still a Schedule IV substance, the legal consequences are the same as those associated with a Schedule I substance.

Substance	DEA Number	Other Names
Furethidine	9626	
Gama Hydroxybutyric Acid (GHB)	2010	GHB, gama hydroxybutyrate, sodium oxybate
Heroin	9200	Diacetylmorphine, diamorphine
Hydromorphinol	9301	
Hydroxypethidine	9627	
Ibogaine	7260	Constituent of "Tabernanthe iboga" plant
Ketobemidone	9628	Cliradon
Levomoramide	9629	
Levophenacylmorphan	9631	
Lysergic acid diethylamide	7315	LSD, lysergide
Marijuana	7360	Cannabis, marijuana
Mecloqualone	2572	Nubarene
Mescaline	7381	Constituent of "Peyote" cacti

This table shows a portion of Schedule I controlled substances in the United States. According to U.S. laws, none of these drugs has a legally accepted medical use. However, like Rohypnol, some drugs included in Schedule I are used legally in other countries.

The DEA is now considering removing Rohypnol from Schedule IV and adding it to Schedule I. (The club drug GHB was reclassified in 2000 as a Schedule I drug due to its high potential for abuse.) Drugs under Schedule I are thought to have no proven benefit in medical treatment and are not considered safe, even under medical supervision. In 2006, Schedule I drugs included LSD and heroin, among others. At the state level, Florida, Idaho, Minnesota, New Hampshire, New Mexico, North Dakota, Oklahoma, and Pennsylvania already classify Rohypnol as a Schedule I drug. This classification increases the penalties for possession, use, and distribution of the drug.

THE ECSTASY ANTI-PROLIFERATION ACT

In chapter 2, Karen was fortunate to get help with her recovery from drug addiction. Some teens are not so lucky, and they end up making choices that have many negative consequences. They may find themselves living on the street, or they may get arrested and go to jail. Some may have to live with permanent brain damage or a serious illness for the rest of their lives. Others may

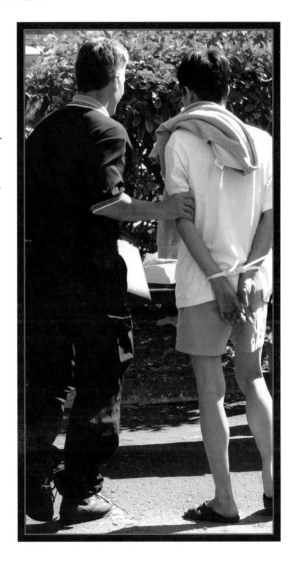

A Drug Enforcement Administration agent (left) arrests a suspected ecstasy dealer in March 2004. Dealing club drugs brings with it legal consequences that are becoming more and more serious.

even lose their lives as a result of their drug use. If Karen had continued on her drug-abusing path, she could have easily ended up dealing drugs herself. If she had been arrested and convicted of selling ecstasy, she would have faced many years in prison. The Ecstasy Anti-Proliferation Act, passed by Congress in 2000, makes it a serious crime to distribute ecstasy. The law increased sentences for distributing 800 pills (approximately 200 grams) of ecstasy from fifteen months to five years. It also increased the penalties of distributing 8,000 pills from forty-one months to ten years.

THE ECSTASY PREVENTION ACT

On its Web site, the Drug Abuse Warning Network (DAWN) shows how dramatically ecstasy use was rising in the late 1990s.

U.S. Customs agent James Burke inspects bags containing about 172,000 illegal ecstasy pills, seized in April 2000. The huge profits made from selling illegal club drugs attract an endless supply of dealers. The street value of these drugs was estimated at $4.5 million.

DAWN notes that in 1997, ecstasy was mentioned in 637 hospital emergency room visits in the United States. In 2001, the number rose to 5,542. In light of the ecstasy threat, in 2002, Congress signed into law the Ecstasy Prevention Act. This legislation outlined specific steps to reduce the trafficking, distribution, and abuse of ecstasy and other club drugs, including Rohypnol. It also led to funding for educational programs to alert young people to the risks and health effects of ecstasy. For example, in 2002, Congress allocated $15 million to combat the spread of ecstasy and other club drugs in high-traffic areas. In addition, $1 million was allocated for the National Institute on Drug Abuse to evaluate the effects of ecstasy on an individual's health. The Ecstasy Prevention Act also provides funding for programs to educate health-care professionals and law enforcement agencies regarding the growing problem of ecstasy use and trafficking.

OPERATION X-OUT

In 2002, the DEA further increased its anti–club drug efforts by launching Operation X-Out. This program focused on the problem of club and date rape drugs in the United States and in other countries. Operation X-Out was designed to educate the public about the dangers of ecstasy, Rohypnol, GHB, and ketamine, as well as to identify the organizations that produce and distribute these drugs.

CHAPTER 5

Drug Abuse and Society: What Are the Costs?

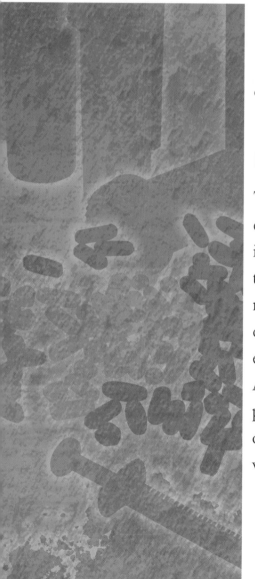

Drug abuse clearly has many negative effects for drug users and their families. It also adversely affects the economy and society in many ways.

MONEY WELL SPENT?

The U.S. government spends billions of tax dollars every year to decrease drug trafficking and provide drug prevention and treatment programs. Despite these efforts, recent statistics show that illegal drug use continues to be a widespread problem. For example, the 2005 National Drug Threat Assessment reported that almost 35 million people who were twelve years of age or older used an illegal drug during the previous year. The assessment, which is compiled by the National Drug Intelligence Center, also stated that about four million people were dependent on or abused illegal drugs in 2003.

The Substance Abuse and Mental Health Services Administration, a U.S. government agency, conducts the annual National Survey on Drug Use and Health. According to the 2005 survey, marijuana was the most common illegal drug, used by 14.6 million people older than age twelve. The survey also revealed that two million people over the age of twelve were cocaine users. In addition, nearly 930,000 people used hallucinogens such as LSD, and an estimated 166,000 people used heroin.

THE HIGH COST OF DRUG TRAFFICKING

The high demand for illegal drugs in the United States has created one of the most profitable drug trafficking markets in the world. To feed the demand, criminal organizations around the globe produce, smuggle, and distribute large amounts of drugs, including cocaine, heroin, marijuana, and methamphetamine. In the United States alone, income generated by the illegal drug trade amounts to between $100 billion and $200 billion each year. As this chapter explains, the costs of using the drugs, in turn, are passed on to individuals, families, communities, and governments around the world.

Drug dealing is a dirty business, conducted in the shadows and behind closed doors. Dealers do not care about the health and safety of the people who buy their drugs. Dealers would have a much harder time peddling their wares if they warned buyers of the risks involved in using their products.

INDIVIDUALS AND THE HIGH PRICE OF DRUG ABUSE

Drug use invites a host of problems into a person's life. Users often have unstable relationships with friends and family members. Fatigue and distraction caused by drug use may lead to poor job performance, which may lead to the loss of a job and income. Drug users often have unhealthy diets and fail to take

44

proper care of their bodies. As a result, they tend to be sick more frequently than non-users. In addition, drug use is known to lead to poor judgment in sexual affairs, increasing the incidence of AIDS and other sexually transmitted diseases. Due to poor physical and mental health, drug users may become dependent on others for both emotional and financial support. Unable to live independently and make smart choices, they lose the ability to be active, productive members of society.

Illegal addictive drugs are often expensive. The high cost of maintaining a habit may lead a person to commit such crimes as robbery, prostitution, or drug trafficking. This increases the likelihood that a drug user will get arrested or go to jail. Most users don't think of themselves as criminals, but it is their demand for drugs that fuels the lucrative illegal drug trafficking trade. The highly competitive and dangerous lifestyle of individuals involved in drug trafficking leads to violent crimes. Often, the victims of these crimes are the drug users themselves.

It is estimated that 65 percent of all prisoners in the United States are incarcerated for drug-related offenses. The average cost per year to feed, clothe, and provide shelter for an inmate is $20,674. Moreover, state corrections officials estimate that between 70 percent and 85 percent of inmates will need some level of substance-abuse treatment. The rising costs of rehabilitating drug users both in and out of prison are a serious burden for government agencies. According to the 2004 National Survey on Drug Use and Health, 3.8 million people age twelve or older had received treatment within the past twelve months for a drug or alcohol problem.

NATIONAL DRUG CONTROL STRATEGY

In 1989, the White House Office of National Drug Control Policy established the National Drug Control Strategy to deal with the increase of drug abuse in America. This strategy proposed a long-term plan to reduce illegal drug use by 50 percent by 2007. The proposal is aimed at prevention, treatment, research, law enforcement, protection of U.S. borders, and working cooperatively with other countries.

The funding levels for the National Drug Control Strategy are set up according to three key priorities.

This young drug suspect is behind bars in a detention facility, waiting to be taken to jail. Since 1989, U.S. cities have received funding to be more aggressive in fighting drug trafficking. This has produced more arrests, but preventing and treating drug addiction remain difficult issues to solve.

Economic Costs

This table shows historical funding for the Office of National Drug Control Policy (ONDCP) to carry out the National Drug Control Strategy. (Dollar figures in billions.)

Fiscal Year	2000 (Final)	2001 (Final)	2002 (Final)	2003 (Final)	2004 (Final)	2005 (Final)	2006 (Enacted)	2007 (Requested)
Total	$9.936	$9.467	$10.646	$11.083	$11.867	$12.642	$12.546	$12.655

These include establishing drug prevention programs, designing treatment strategies, and taking specific steps to reduce the availability of illegal drugs. As you can see from the chart above, the total projected budget for the program in 2007 is $12.655 billion. This is nearly $109 million more than the 2006 budget. The increased funding will be used for continued reinforcement of specific programs and new initiatives in each of the three high-priority areas. In the years beyond 2007, it is certain that U.S. taxpayers will continue spending billions of dollars each year for prevention and treatment of drug abuse.

CHAPTER 6
Rohypnol and Public Awareness

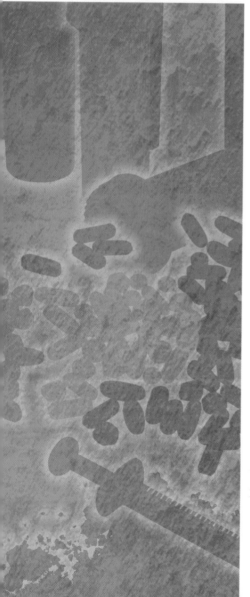

In the late 1990s, the increasing use of date rape drugs in the United States brought about many changes in public attitudes and awareness. Through the media—books, newspapers, magazines, Internet, television, movies, and radio—women were informed of ways to avoid being victims of drug-facilitated sexual assault. In addition, the news media regularly reported on cases of Rohypnol abuse in cities and towns across the United States in an effort to raise awareness among the general public. Educators and support groups, too, responded with their own campaigns to educate young women about Rohypnol and drug-facilitated sexual assault. More recently, these campaigns have included information on GHB and ketamine as well.

THE MEDIA AND THE MESSAGE

The crime of sexual assault is a threat to public welfare. In this sense, it is the responsibility of all citizens to work toward reducing it. Experienced rape crisis counselors say that access to accurate and balanced information is one of the key factors in preventing drug-facilitated sexual assaults. Sometimes, the most powerful information is the most personal information. The campaigns for awareness are often led by women of all ages who themselves have been victimized. Although their stories are often very painful, these women have used the various media to try to make sure that what happened to them never happens to anyone else.

WATCH YOUR DRINK—WATCH YOUR FRIENDS

Printed materials such as posters, fliers, and stickers have been useful in warning women of the dangers of date rape drugs. In 2001, the Crime Victims Foundation, the Sexual Assault and Domestic Violence Center, and the Women's Resource Center at California State University, Sacramento, teamed up to promote awareness of these dangerous drugs. Called "Watch Your Drink—Watch Your Friends," the campaign helped to educate women on college campuses in Sacramento and Yolo County, California. Informative stickers and posters were placed in college dorms to warn of the effects of date rape drugs. In

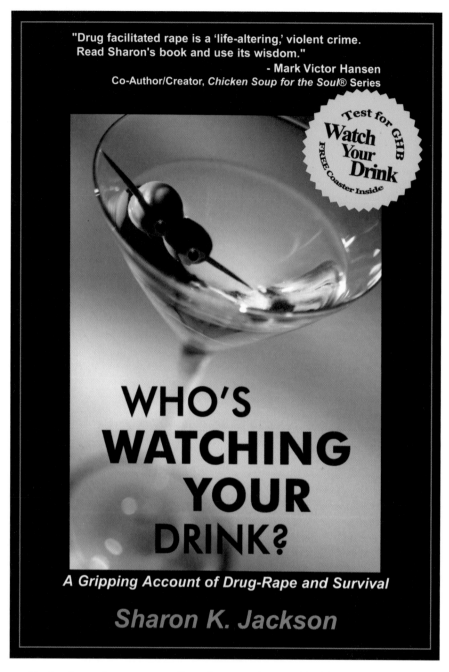

"Drug facilitated rape is a 'life-altering,' violent crime. Read Sharon's book and use its wisdom."
- Mark Victor Hansen
Co-Author/Creator, *Chicken Soup for the Soul*® Series

Test for GHB
Watch Your Drink
FREE Coaster Inside

WHO'S WATCHING YOUR DRINK?

A Gripping Account of Drug-Rape and Survival

Sharon K. Jackson

Sharon K. Jackson began a national campaign called Project Watch Your Drink to educate and support victims of drug-facilitated sexual assault. She also wrote *Who's Watching Your Drink? (shown here)* to tell about her personal experience with the date rape drug GHB. She hopes that by sharing her story, she can prevent others from becoming victims.

addition, informational drink coasters were sent to several bars in the area. The groups hoped that these efforts would make students aware of the potential danger posed by men who might slip a date rape drug into their drink. The program was a success, as the participating bars soon had to ask for more coasters and napkins to replace the ones students took to share with friends when they left the bar.

These young women are using special coasters to test their drinks for the presence of a date rape drug. The makers of this coaster claim that their product works 95 percent of the time. However, law enforcement experts say the coasters alone cannot prevent drug-facilitated sexual assaults.

The success of the "Watch Your Drink–Watch Your Friends" campaign led to television reports that sparked further awareness around the country. In December 2003, the Centers for Disease Control and Prevention teamed up with the Florida Department of Health to send out one million "Watch Your Drink" cocktail napkins to bars and clubs across Florida. The napkins also included Web site information and phone numbers for the Florida Council Against Sexual Violence.

Prevention Strategies Are Working

Rohypnol education strategies seem to be succeeding in reducing the use of the drug in sexual assaults. In 2002, an Australian company introduced testing strips that change color when they come into contact with a liquid that has been spiked. The strips are designed to detect GHB and ketamine, but not Rohypnol. Why not Rohypnol? According to the inventors of the strips, Rohypnol is no longer the criminal's drug of choice for spiking drinks.

TEN FACTS ABOUT ROHYPNOL

1. Rohypnol is the trade name for flunitrazepam, a strong tranquilizer that is illegal in the United States.
2. Popular club drugs taken at dance parties and all-night raves include ecstasy, GHB, ketamine, and Rohypnol. All are potentially dangerous.

3. Drug trafficking in the United States brings in an estimated annual income of between $100 and $200 billion for organized crime.

4. In 2006, the U.S. government budgeted more than $12.5 billion for drug prevention programs, drug treatment strategies, and efforts to reduce drug trafficking.

5. Rohypnol, ketamine, and GHB have been targeted as the three drugs most often used in drug-facilitated sexual assaults.

6. The Drug-Induced Rape Prevention and Punishment Act (1996) increased penalties for anyone giving a controlled substance to a person without his or her consent for the purpose of committing a violent crime.

7. Rohypnol is known as the "forget-me pill" because it typically causes memory loss of events that happened while under its influence.

8. Since 1997, some batches of Rohypnol pills have been manufactured in such a way that they turn liquids blue to alert a potential victim that a drink has been spiked.

9. A woman who thinks she may have been given Rohypnol and sexually assaulted should contact the police or rape crisis center immediately for help.

10. Women should never leave a drink unattended in a bar or at a party. They should work together to protect themselves and their friends from the dangers of date rape drugs.

IN CONCLUSION

Rohypnol is the trade name for the synthetic drug flunitrazepam. It is a sedative in the benzodiazepine family of drugs. Doctors in Europe and Latin America may prescribe Rohypnol to treat sleep and anxiety disorders. However, Rohypnol is—and always has been—illegal in the United States. Until the mid-1990s, it was relatively easy to import Rohypnol into the United States across the U.S.-Mexico border. However, Rohypnol became increasingly popular as a club drug, and reports of its widespread abuse came to light. As a result, the U.S. government passed legislation to increase penalties for its possession, use, and distribution. The recreational use of Rohypnol and other club drugs continues to be a major concern in the United States. In addition to harming the bodies and brains of those who use them, these illegal drugs are a huge burden on American taxpayers.

Rohypnol acts quickly and may cause blackouts and memory loss. Some criminals slip the drug into the drink of an unsuspecting victim to facilitate a sexual attack. One of the key steps in addressing the problem of drug-facilitated sexual assault is to educate the public about the dangers of the drugs used in this type of assault. To meet this need, a growing number of educational programs have been developed at the local, state, and national levels. These programs offer information on how to identify the drug and its effects. Armed with this knowledge, potential victims can better protect themselves and their friends. For those who have been assaulted and need help, there are many resources available that offer specific information about what to do and whom to contact. Authorities hope that with stronger penalties against potential abusers, as well as the increased awareness of potential victims, the impact of illegal drugs like Rohypnol will continue to decline.

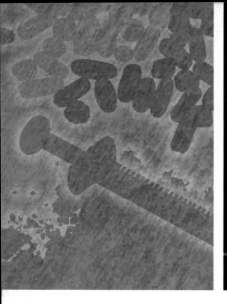

GLOSSARY

amnesia Partial or complete loss of memory as a result of brain injury, illness, or drug use.

anesthetic A substance that causes loss of consciousness or feeling in the body.

anxiety A feeling combining worry, nervousness, and fear.

blackout Loss of consciousness.

depressant A drug that slows down the functioning of the central nervous system.

facilitate To make something easier.

hallucination The perception of objects or noises that do not exist in reality.

intoxicate To cause drunkenness through alcohol or drugs.

legislation Laws; rules that have the force of official authority.

overdose Too high a dose of a medicine or drug.

paralysis Loss of feeling in, or the ability to move, a body part.

prosecute To carry out a court action against someone in order to enforce the law.

spike To add something to a drink.

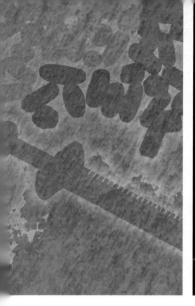

FOR MORE INFORMATION

Drug Enforcement
  Administration (DEA)
Mailstop: AES
2401 Jefferson Davis Highway
Alexandria, VA 22301
(202) 307-1000
Web site: http://
  www.usdoj.gov/dea

National Center for Victims
  of Crime
2000 M Street NW,
  Suite 480
Washington, DC 20036
(202) 467-8700
Web site: http://
  www.ncvc.org

National Criminal Justice
  Reference Service (NCJRS)
P.O. Box 6000
Rockville, MD 20849-6000
(800) 851-3420
Web site: http://www.ncjrs.
  gov/spotlight/club_drugs/
  legislation.html

National Institute on Drug
  Abuse (NIDA)
National Institutes of Health
6001 Executive Boulevard,
  Room 5213
Bethesda, MD 20892-9561
Web site: http://
  www.nida.nih.gov

The National Women's Health Information Center
U.S. Department of Health and Human Services
Office on Women's Health
(800) 994-9662
Web site: http://www.4woman.gov/faq/rohypnol.htm

Rape, Abuse and Incest National Network (RAINN)
2000 L Street NW, Suite 406
Washington, DC 20036
Hotline: (800) 656-HOPE

Web site: http://www.rainn.org

WEB SITES:

Due to the changing nature of Internet links, the Rosen Publishing Group, Inc., has developed an online list of Web sites related to the subject of this book. This site is updated regularly. Please use this link to access the list:

http://www.rosenlinks.com/das/rohy

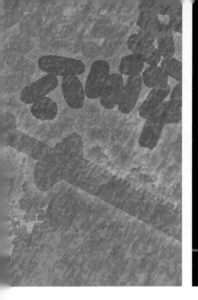

FOR FURTHER READING

Kehner, George. *Date Rape Drugs.* Philadelphia, PA: Chelsea House Publishers, 2004.

Landau, Elaine. *Date Violence.* New York, NY: Franklin Watts, 2004.

Marcovitz, Hal. *Club Drugs.* San Diego, CA; Lucent Books, 2006.

Robbins, Paul R. *Designer Drugs.* Springfield, NJ: Enslow Publishers, 1995.

Tattersall, Clare. *Date Rape Drugs.* New York, NY: Rosen Publishing Group, Inc., 2000.

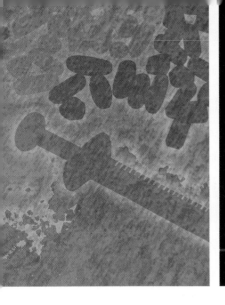

BIBLIOGRAPHY

Balkin, Karen F., ed. *Club Drugs*. Farmington Hills, MI: Greenhaven Press, 2005.

Clayton, Lawrence, Ph.D. *Designer Drugs*, rev. ed. New York, NY: Rosen Publishing Group, Inc., 1998.

Leshner, Alan I. "Club Drugs Aren't Fun Drugs." National Institute on Drug Abuse. Retrieved February 2006 (http://www.drugabuse.gov/Published_Articles/fundrugs.html).

Maxwell, Jane Carlisle. "Party Drugs: Properties, Prevalence, Patterns, and Problems." *Substance Use and Misuse*, Vol. 40: pp. 1,203–1,240, 2005.

Monitoring the Future. "2005 Data From In-School Surveys of 8th-, 10th-, and 12th-Grade Students." Retrieved January 2006 (http://www.monitoringthefuture.org/data/05data.html).

National Institute on Drug Abuse (NIDA). "NIDA InfoFacts: High School and Youth Trends." December 2004. Retrieved January 2006 (http://www.nida.nih.gov/infofacts/HSYouthtrends.html).

National Institute on Drug Abuse (NIDA). "NIDA InfoFacts: Rohypnol and GHB." March 2005. Retrieved January 2006 (http://www.nida.nih.gov/Infofacts/RohypnolGHB.html).

Office of National Drug Control Policy (ONDCP). "Drug Treatment in the Criminal Justice System." March 2001. Retrieved January 2006 (http://www.whitehousedrugpolicy.gov/publications/factsht/treatment).

Porrata, Trinka. "DFSA: Growing Concern But Training Sadly Lacking." Project GHB. Retrieved February 2006 (http://www.projectghb.org/rape/dfsa.htm).

Rape, Abuse and Incest National Network (RAINN). "Helping Yourself, Helping Others." Retrieved January 2006 (http://www.rainn.org/what-should-i-do/index.html).

Sorentrue, Heather. "Watch Your Drink Campaign." WCJB-TV20 News. December 18, 2003. Retrieved January 2006 (http://www.wcjb.com/news.asp?id=8815).

Substance Abuse & Mental Health Services Administration (SAMSHA). "National Survey on Drug Use and Health." March 10, 2006. Retrieved March 2006 (http://www.oas.samhsa.gov/NSDUH.htm#NSDUHinfo).

U.S. Drug Enforcement Administration. "Drug Trafficking in the United States." Retrieved March 2006 (http://www.usdoj.gov/dea/concern/drug_trafficking.html).

U.S. Drug Enforcement Administration. "Flunitrazepam (Rohypnol)." Retrieved January 2006 (http://www.usdoj.gov/dea/pubs/rohypnol/rohypnol.htm).

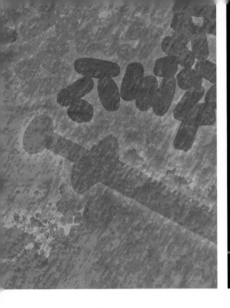

INDEX

ABOUT THE AUTHOR

Colleen Adams is a former special education teacher of elementary and middle school students. She has written numerous volumes for Rosen Publishing Group, Inc. As a teacher and a mother of teenage children, she is interested in educational research and materials that help young people learn about the dangers of drugs.

PHOTO CREDITS